The Cry of a
Mother's Heart

The Cry of a
Mother's Heart

Poems by Rebecca K. Pinker
Illustrations by Jana E. Pinker

Rebecca K. Pinker

3·9·06

Jana completed the painting used as the cover on November 9, 1998. She passed away November 23, 1998. Jana called this Riches.

ISBN: 1-58597-274-6

Library of Congress Control Number: 2004094031

LEATHERS
PUBLISHING

A division of Squire Publishers, Inc.
4500 College Blvd.
Leawood, KS 66211
1-888-888-7696
www.leatherspublishing.com

in memory of Jana

I write this book in memory of my daughter, Jana, who died at the age of nineteen. I dedicate this book to all parents and siblings who survive the death of a child and to others who experience the death of a loved one. I believe that we all make the same journey, moving to dawn.

Reader,

My words have life because of you —
you say them in your mind
then they are there — real —
real for you. Perhaps not
the same real as for me.
But because you read my words,
you make my poem.

— RKP

CONTENTS

Daylight

Dark Night

Near Dawn

ACKNOWLEDGEMENTS

This book has been in progress during the years since Jana's death, November 23, 1998. Several months after Jana died, I found a letter in her room that she had written to me the previous summer. In the letter, she stated: "Mom, I want you to publish a book." Well, Jana, here's the book.

I am thankful for my other children and my husband: Jonathan, Jennifer, and Bob. I have felt their confidence in and support of my work throughout this journey. They have helped me to continue on when the darkness surrounded me.

I owe much gratitude to Virgil Albertini, Ph.D., George Day, Ph.D., and Bob Xidis, Ph.D., who provided invaluable insight and showed great patience as they examined my work. They are not only my readers but also my treasured colleagues and friends.

I am grateful to Billy Spindle, Jana's fifth grade teacher. She encouraged and guided Jana to create and to experience her feelings through art. As well, I greatly value Jana's art therapist from Kansas City Hospice, Laura Aube. She helped Jana express the essence of life in the midst of dying.

I am profoundly thankful for the two kindred spirits that have come into my life since Jana died. Without their encouragement, my words would still be silent.

Finally, I want to thank Mollie Eulitt, my editor at Leathers Publishing, for walking with me through the publishing process — at my pace — and for helping me to make my book a reality.

PROLOGUE

The death of a child occurs out of life's sequence; no matter what age the parent, the death of a child is out of life's order. When such a death happens, the world seems to stop; then, when it begins again, the world has a different color, and life has a different meaning.

Jana Elizabeth Pinker graduated from high school in May 1997. Three months later Jana was diagnosed with a rare form of liver cancer. At the M.D. Anderson Cancer Research Center, Houston, we learned that she would live twelve to twenty-four months. Jana lived fifteen months. She died on November 23, 1998, at the age of nineteen.

Jana's artwork in this book traces her years from preschool through post high school. Jana did the watercolor paintings found on the cover and on section pages while working with Laura Aube. The cover painting, Jana titled *Riches*. The flowers stand for complete peace; her understanding of going to heaven; her thankfulness for her relationships; and her thankfulness for her faith. The hand represents each family member. She drew a symbol of her tumor in the lower right corner. Jana painted cornstalks in the second watercolor. This painting represents her love for her grandparents, their farm, and the closeness she felt to them. She said that she looked forward to meeting her grandma in heaven.

Four weeks before Jana died, she had a near-death experience. When she woke from a coma, she had a renewed exuberance for life. Jana lived each day to the fullest. Several days after her hospital stay, Jana wanted to take a drive to see the fall foliage; it was especially beautiful that year. As we sat in quietness imprinting the colorful maples in our minds forever, Jana held my hand. Tears fell from my eyes; she smiled and said to me: "Mom, let it be." That moment was one of deep understanding without explanation. We both knew her death was coming, but I never fathomed the devastation that I would feel when it came. I have written these pieces since Jana's death as I try to survive this terrible loss. The words are my cry.

Daylight

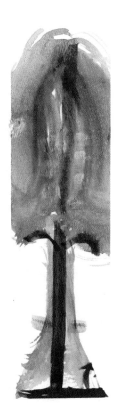

The Current

like a flowing river,
words tumble over words,
a comma, a dash, a space — afloat,
wondering where to rest.

a waterfall these words create
if only now on paper thin —
the rapid force comes from the heart;
the hand swims slower, a clumsy start.

where will the bubbling words end up?
a reservoir, a dried creek bed?
in time the current will wash away
meandering thoughts in switchbacks

or be dammed up.

Ordinary Days

Ordinary days are
the best days
when I can
paint upon
life's mural the
insignificant
and the plain that
color the corners
and paint the borders.
So when I view
the painting,
some time hence,
I see the
glorious beauty
of ordinary days.

Autumn Whisper

From books I know about two roads;
I know that God can make a tree.
But who can climb or who can roam
The God-made tree or the road to see?

Trees dress in autumn's vast array,
Like a painter's palette, from afar.
No spell can make such beauty stay;
This splendor fades like evening's star.

Yet, I can climb each glorious tree,
In springtime's green or autumn's red,
Or walk a wooded path with ease —
Such thoughts, like silk, in memory threads.

What lies within creates the path
Of yellow wood or climbing trees.
These spots of nature ever last;
The soul finds peace in quays like these.

Broken Pieces

After an ice storm,
Heavy arms hang from trees.
They glisten and crack,
Cold enamel hard.

The shiny glaze pulls
Branches to earth.
They snap and fall.
Broken trees, broken spirits.

Tree arms stacked along
The roadside wait for trash trucks.
Their lives end too soon
Because of ice storms.

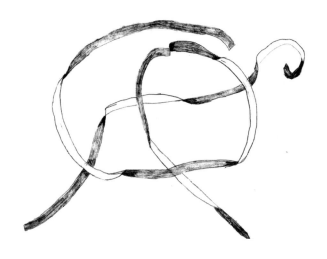

Spring Fantasy

It's spring again, and I have
an attraction for the nymphs
who sprinkle sweet scents
and dust the flowers with
fragrances. Such springtime
fairies mesmerize and hypnotize.
I see their gold, green, blue,
and celebrate each newness.
They make me see beauty
for awhile. Yet, spring abates
with each passing moment.

Why can't the nymphs stay
near forever?

Jennifer Pinker

The Park – Across the Way

Sitting in the breeze with
Thoughts of other days,
I watch a little girl mount
A merry-go-round.
She goes round and round
Spinning as fast as she can.
A little boy on a swing
Goes higher and higher
Pumping his skinny legs.
The spring breeze blows:
"Blow them along."
For them, the day
Ahead stretches long.
"Little girl, Little boy,
Put this day in your pocket.
When the wind dies down,
The merry-go-round rests,
The swing slows,
In the twilight
Touch your pocket.
This day is there."

August's Actuality

August, you are a trickster,
Fooling us to think you are a new beginning.
With unopened boxes of pencils and crayons,
Lined slick white paper,
In wire-bound notebooks,
You make us think of new chances.

August, you are a deceiver;
You bring brown parched grass,
Thirsty dry-leaf trees,
Withered tomato vines,
Shriveled un-ripened pumpkins.

August, your new hope lies
As diminished as yesterday's garden.
And new beginnings are
Only faded "what ifs."

Who Are You?

Gazing at your facade,
I wonder who you are.
Where have you been?
Where do you travel? In
the sequence of life — too
short, too small — you follow
a course unmarked.

Purple Rage

In blue sandals, showing Purple Rage polish,
her feet stepped sluggishly over the burning blacktop,
carefully, one foot in front of the other.

Then a pebble, a pop-top,
a twisted ankle, or some aspect of illness,
and her world tumbled.

With arms outstretched, she grabbed the air.
As bones bounced on the asphalt,
her sun glasses landed under a hip.

Her legs sprawled — one forward, one back;
broken glass pierced her palms;
dark spots dotted the pavement.

Slowly, she stood; abrasions turned from pink
to purple with streaks of crimson;
tiny stones embedded her flesh.

As hands trembled, her voice cracked:
"I really am OK; it's just my
favorite pair of sunglasses — busted!"

Two Friends

How are you doing?
> Great.

What's going on?
> I'm working on a crossword puzzle.
> What's the name of a river in Italy
> that Julius Caesar crossed? Seven letters,
> I think. Oh, and I'm taking chemo;
> my hair's falling out.

Oh, gosh. Well, have you seen any good movies?
> Yeah, two great ones. In the first one, the girl
> wants her boy friend to take out her best friend;
> then the best friend dies of cancer. The second
> one is really funny. Two girls get ready for
> their ten-year high school reunion. They try
> to make a big impression.

Wow! We just graduated. I can't imagine our reunion.
> Me, either, but, you know
> I will never live to see my first reunion.
> I wonder what impression I have made.

Nineteen

We filled the afternoons
reading Bernie Siegel and
Chicken Soup, drinking lemonade —
pink and yellow.
She seemed thirty-five,
though only nineteen.

Evening came; we sat on
the veranda and watched
the moon rise through the maple tree;
we listened to the crickets.
We talked of places far away:
places she had seen;
places she wanted to see.
She was nineteen.

Late night, lying on her bed,
above, on the ceiling,
constellations glowed.
She told each name to me while
the hall clock chimed downstairs.
All she knew was nineteen.

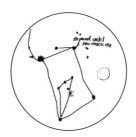

An Opened Door

The hardest thing I have ever
done was open my door —
open my door to a nurse
who came to see my daughter,
my teenage daughter.

To her friend, my daughter stated
the simple fact: Today, a Hospice
nurse came to see me; you know
what that means, don't you?

We all knew what it meant.

Dark Night

They Were Right

They were right, the Old Masters, about suffering.

As we sit here, watching the rain and
eating currant scones, somewhere in a home,
in a hospital someone awaits death:
separation and loss.

And we eat our breakfast food
thinking of our day's plans,
a stream of consciousness:
wondering and anticipating.

The November rain drums on;
the breakfast dishes clatter;
the radio station plays oldies:
the sixties' and the eighties.'

They were right, the Old Masters, about death.

The Crab

pencil legs —
knobby knees, swollen —
in my own mind
such a truth,
that's what i thought.

pussy-willow head
with locks buzzed off —
a shorn sheep —
facial features
magnified.

strong will and fiery
eyes penetrated life
and glimpsed
a look beyond —
that's what i saw.

in ancient days
Theodora felt the
same crab creep
into her breast.
her fight raged on.

five forty-eight A.D.
the crab took over.
nineteen ninety-eight
the crab won the war.
that's what i know.

Beep, Beep, Beep

I have done the watching and the waiting.
I have heard the monitor beeping, breaking
the night with the sound of life.

I have seen eye lids flutter with the pull
to darkness greater than the pull to light,
a purple hue coloring the tissue.

I have touched chalky skin loosely covering
blue veins and wondered where did
last summer's tan go.

I have seen Stillness creeping down the hall
and through the door, climbing up on the bed
to stay. Stillness sat so quietly

and in silence said: "I am here waiting
just like you." What did Stillness
know that I didn't?

Beep.

Wild Geese Call

Early morning,
I see the wild geese
Overhead. As I sit,
I watch these birds
Swing their formation
Wide then narrow,
But always spear-shaped ^.
The wild geese — with heads
Straight, bodies sleek —
Soar easily skyward.
The wild geese call:
Fly with us,
Join our flock,
Float through the clouds.
Come, catch the wild wind.

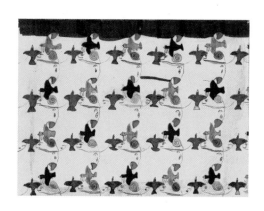

Jana's Song

I may die, but that is all I will do for death.
I will paint my picture on life's backdrop.
I will sing a song of independence.
I will walk for those too feeble or too weighed down.
I will do what others only dream of doing.
I may die, but that is all I will do for death.
I will pick spring's first dandelions and make
a priceless necklace.
I will smell the new cut grass on summer's lawn.
I will make shadow pictures in the sun's golden rays.
I will catch June's first lightning bugs and watch
as they light up my world.
I may die, but that is all I will do for death.
I will live now and live on in the memories of others.
I will dance to the songs of angels.
I will be seen in each billowy cloud.
I will be felt when night breezes sing softly,
and I will be reflected in each full moon.
I may die, but that is all I will do for death.

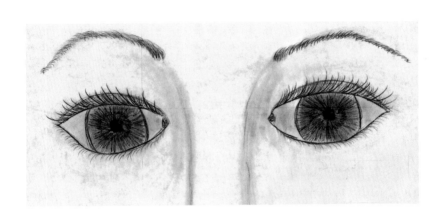

Epiphany

air bites of the coming change
while crisp blueness touches heaven.
leaves blush their varied shades;
fence rows host comely stalks.

a caravan of darkness moves
unobtrusively amid nature's
exuberance, snailing toward
its destination.

a solitary well-worn car approaches
from the east, he on his side.
the driver, worn as well,
pulls sideward off the road, then stops.

as the procession passes,
he pauses, lifts his hat
and places it across his chest;
reverently he bows his head.

he does not know who rests
within the train; it does
not matter. his gesture comes
so clearly; it seems to say:

rest in peace for the beloved,
that is understood; and for
those who remain, they rest
in God's peace as well.

Yesterday

Yesterday, Death
stalked my home
and found his prey.

He came uninvited,
stealing my confidence,
optimism and denial.

Advancing before
dawn, between the layers
of belief and unbelief,

He drew close
with devouring teeth
and raking claws,

Ready to slash
the beating
chambers of my heart.

He pounced with claws
clutching, fangs flaring, breath
stinking, flesh rotting.

Death came,
all for his hunger
to be satisfied.

Shards of Pain

i want to break a substantial piece of glass:
a goblet, a light bulb, a mirror.
smash the glass with my hand
on the side where back meets front,
where pain and flow would be great.

i want the jagged edges to pulsate rapidly
spilling, flowing, dripping unceasingly.
feel the shards cut deeply into my hand,
feel the penetration of each fragmented piece.
i want to feel the uncontrollable throb,
the sick, queasiness that invades the stomach,
the lightheadedness that makes breathing
shallow and guarded.

i want to see the blood as it spurts swiftly
between the slices of flesh.
watch as the blood drips on my jeans,
as the denim absorbs the sticky red stuff.
t h e n, maybe t h e n, the pain outside might
momentarily cover the pain within.

Sink

sink.
sink.
blackness
come,
cover
me up.
the abyss
calls me.
I fall a
familiar
fall; this
time
I welcome
it —
I know
the way.
too soon
I try to
climb the
slippery
sorrowful
sides,
making
my way
upward.

I want
to stay
on the
bottom.

Sea of Red, Rush of Purple

I try to translate my silence,
tell of my world apart from here.
I try to speak to a world that does
not hear. For my words are a
sea of red and a rush of purple;
they flow without restraint;
they flow without composure,
and they find power in the unsaid.

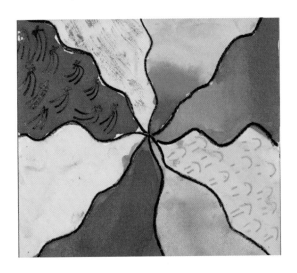

Alone in God's World

Alone in God's world,
Coolness settles on my shoulders.
Dew glistens on short green spikes.
But only for a while, for winter comes.
I listen for God's voice,
But I hear only a bird singing,
A stream running,
A coyote calling.

When will I hear God's voice?

The Death of a Child

a child —
a treasure
of greatest joy —
when gone
a wound that
will not heal
nor would I
have it so.

Powerless

Life spins,
and I am tangled
in its threads.

Life engulfs,
and I am smothered
in its arms.

Life devours,
and I am caught
in vicious teeth.

Life cuts,
and I am bleeding
in my soul.

Gray Mist

He came to call clothed in a gray felt hat;
The evening's eyes covered by the cool mist.
He didn't stay long, but for a while he sat;
Insistently, he took without a risk,

Stealing, plucking away a precious load —
An innocent he felt that he had bought —
Without regard for status on life's road;
He brought no word of comfort or kind thought.

Not him, the dim cold mist, he brought the night.
He came softly, quickly, a false beauty,
Sadness, chaos, only — no ray of light.
He left anger and bold temerity.

Gray Mist! I wonder why that night you came,
Changing my life, never to be the same.

Grief Known

So, what do you know of grief?
Come, walk with me awhile.
Come to her grave where green
Grass thickens in the spring loam,
Dandelions reflect her countenance,
Birds sing their melodious tunes.
Where the hope of resurrection lingers,
Yet, absence is understood far better
Than a heavenly resting place.
Come, walk with me in loneliness,
Then, tell me you know grief.

O God Our Help In Ages Past

I took God so for granted
Before I knew death's timelessness.
My mother said He walked with me —
That I could hear Him talk,
That I could feel Him near.
Then, she went to be with Jesus,
So, it was God and me, alone.

As children came,
I told them grandma's words.
"God walks with us and talks with us,
 and you can feel Him near as well."
And they believed as I believed.

One day, one child —
She went to be with Jesus.
Now, I walk and talk alone.
I walk the path and feel no presence —
I talk in solitude and hear no voice —
Where is the God of ages past?

Unwanted Companion

Grief has a way of stepping into my
shoes. It comes to walk wherever I go.
Sometimes it pinches my toes.

 My feet don't like this extra
companion; they say that grief
takes up too much room.

Often I think if I change shoes,
I won't feel the grief.
But that's not true.

When I slip my feet into a pair
of running shoes or high heels,
grief slips in as well.

I stretch my toes, wiggle my toes,
stand on tiptoe, walk on my heels —
yet, grief always seems to touch my sole.

As a last resort, I slip my shoes off,
then my socks. I place my feet
on the bed, under the blankets.

Then my feet rest,
and grief seems
to hide in the closet.

Marshmallows and Whipped Cream

I will never again taste the sweetness of marshmallows,
and don't ask me to swallow whipped cream
instead of chicken soup and Jell-O.

Don't push me to ride a rollercoaster when the one
that I'm on has taken me to the depth of darkness,
and the first car struggles on the upward climb.

Don't ask me to sing or make a joyful
noise for my eardrums reverberate a
funeral dirge.

Don't expect me to look to tomorrow
for my today hangs heavy, and the end
of this day seems hopelessly far away.

Just stand beside me and let me find
my own sunshine in the dark clouds above.
For I remember it being there, before.

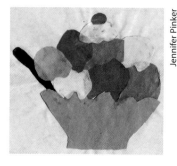

Jennifer Pinker

My Life Closed Twice

Tribute to Emily Dickinson

my life closed twice before,
the poet says aright —
with me on one side, them on the other —
the doors of death closed tight.

the first shut quickly —
I knew not death's great force —
and though the door stood fast —
the crack seeped my remorse.

the second door more slowly shut.
yet, I was not prepared —
this door brought gloom, despair —
before I was aware —

and, now, I wait alone
fumbling in the dark —
me here, them there —
living seems so stark.

will the next door close for me?
the place called heaven
I want to see —
and leave this dark behind.

Jana's Corner

Home from school, right inside
the front door, at the bottom
of the staircase, below the mirror,
she drops her backpack, lunch box,
a pair of shoes and stray hair clips.

Abandoned homework papers
spill from the unzipped pouch
of her backpack cluttering
the floor — so easy to slip on.

Day after day, the same.
Those days when I thought
there would be tomorrows.

Imperfect Rhetoric

How can I put into a poem
the feelings of my heart?
How can I try to rhyme
and have my feeling be just right?
How can I accent words
in strict iambic form?
Will every feeling come
with sound of short then long?
My sense of loneliness seems long
but may not in an iamb fall.
How can I count eight syllables
and then begin another line?
How can I measure grief in each
tetrameter — a cadenced sound?
And what about a poem's tempo?
The grief I have has none.
A rhythm is predictable;
grief knows no constancy.

Stranger in the House

a stranger in the house
a face without a name
a voice without a sound
a labored gasp, it breathes.
a throbbing pulse, a beating heart
a stranger lurks behind the face
but always out of place.
the stranger in my house — is me.

Home

Tribute to Thomas Wolfe

i want to go home,
climb the crooked stairs,
lie atop the bunk,
touch the ceiling
with my bare feet;
to see the light
from the lamp post
gleam in the dark,
and know that night
settles peacefully.
i want to pull
the blankets to my chin
and listen to the rain
drum on the tin
roof overhead,
as lightning brings
shadows to life
in my room and
thunder calls to his mate.
i want darkness
to cover me softly;
to hear the quiet
talk of mom and dad
in the kitchen downstairs,

feel the calm within me.
i want to go back
to a gentler time
when mom and dad
buffered me
from life's wrongs,
when they slew
all my dragons
for me.

I Get Older

Life has gone on; I wanted it to stop.
I wanted the world to be dark and gray,
Like my world when death came.
But the sun came out the very next day.

I wanted to shout and scream:
To tell that my soul cries,
That life is unfair.
But life just went on.

I wanted just one more: year, month —
Just one more of anything;
Willingly, I bargained.
But I was cheated.

As others like me have done,
I ask: how can this be?
But no sound do I hear.
Life just goes on, and I get older.

Lost

I am trying to find God;
I think He's lost.
I've looked for Him in churches and in books;
I've traced His steps to meetings and retreats.
I've felt His shadow in the woods.
But I think God's lost, and
I am trying to find Him.

He wasn't lost when I was twelve.
I met Him at a bible camp.
We sang songs and took walks,
And I knew that I'd found a friend.

Now, I am older and hold grief inside, but
I want to touch the God I knew when I was twelve.
I am trying to find God.
I think He's lost; yet I know —
He's not — I am.

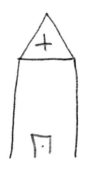

The Sound of Grief

The sound begins as silence:
it's intense, and it keeps getting louder.
I alone can hear it. I panic by the sound.

Others look at me and smile, and they wonder:
What is grief? And I want to tell them about it,
but all I can do is scream in silence.

So silence comes out of my mouth
and my mind, and I smile and wonder
back at them: Why don't you know?

Separation

A stream runs from north to south, cutting back the humus soil,
switching back and forth, east to west. A bridge,
with scattered potholes on the sides from groundhog
diggings, spans the meandering creek.

Upland rhythms help to move the spring freshet
to either side of boulders scattered like pillows
in the stream bed. A fork on down the creek divides pasture
from cornfield; cows graze beside a newly planted field.

She and I stood upon the bridge and looked beyond;
the young fresh stream swept swiftly after torrential rains.
We watched silver-tailed trout swim atop catching bugs;
their gilded tails shimmered in sunlight.

We taped pennies to the underside
of the single-lane bridge, for luck,
always thinking we would return ages on,
and reminisce all that had gone before.

Now I stand alone at the bridge
watching the freshet and the fish
moving swiftly or not at all.
And I feel the boulders that separate us.

The Chair

I want to move that extra chair from
around the table so I'll forget.
But if I remove the chair,
I'm afraid that I won't remember.
That cane-bottom chair held her,
the last to rest upon the seat.
Now it stands alone, close to the table,
but neither quite pushed-in
nor snug under the leaves.
It sets apart, moved away from the closeness
of the oval pine where placemats signal:
one less for dinner tonight.

Barbie Dolls

The sun glimmers through the west window; it illuminates
the yellow walls and warms the gold carpet scattered with doll
clothes. A dollhouse hugs a bright corner;
two little girls orchestrate their fantasies moving dolls
and toy furniture from room to room.

They contrive the future while sitting on the floor
in the sunlight: that moment — the only reality.
The afternoon drifts to early evening
in the golden room: the nights to days.

Now one sits alone; she speaks softly; her words come
slowly, her voice, broken. "I miss playing dolls.
We had so much time back then. I think we'll play again.
If it's a happy place, there must be Barbie dolls in heaven."

Goodbyes

When I was a child, my mom would leave me
for an afternoon. She'd say goodbye,
and I would wander aimlessly from room to room,
missing her. I hated to say goodbye.

As a wife I moved from state to state
with the man I married. We moved farther and farther
away from safety, away from what I'd known.
Leaving, I said so many goodbyes.

When children came, I felt the joy of motherhood
and never dreamed of leavings.
They were forever young, and so was I.
I never thought of saying goodbye.

Not long ago, I said goodbye to one dear child.
She was young and did not want to leave;
I was old and wanted her to stay. She left me
for her heavenly home. I had no choice; I said goodbye.

Though I face each new day,
I struggle with the emptiness that it brings.
Perhaps, I should be happy, for the time we shared,
but I have a problem with goodbyes.

In Another Country

The past is another country,
And I want to travel there,
Go down the coast of consideration
Where the sea's tide rides with care.

Then, journey to the purple fields;
There memories dart in motion
In the heat of summer's day,
The breeze without a notion.

Sea and breeze — another country —
Drifting from the past,
Like phantoms, recede;
My journey never lasts.

Table for Two

I sit in this café
At a table for two.
I read a book
As rain hits the window.
The coffee I drink is hot;
It burns my tongue.
Hands of the clock
Move slowly up
Then down.
Coffee, café, rain, a book —
I recall when two sat at
This table for two.

Bird's Song

Today, I hear the bird sing,
In stillness his clear cry.
His voice stirs up a memory
Of a summer past when
We sat in evening's shade
And watched the pair saunter
Along the porch —

His sound evokes
The time of then,
The song they sang,
His mate and him.
But, now, he is alone
Just like me.

Moving On

Someone said to me:
"I'm glad to see that you've moved on."

And I responded:
"Moved on? With grief, I don't move on.

Those words convey a change,
a leaving behind.

For me, rather,
I move through my grief.

I've come a long way. I may have far
to travel; I may have only a short distance.

I won't know until I see Him and her.
Then, I will have moved on."

She Stands

She stands with
Arms outstretched
Blessed Mother
Such a reminder
Of suffering
Holy Mary
Mother of God

Friend

Friend, where can I
find a soul who knows
my name? Where can I
find one who hears my
song? Dear Friend, where
can I find a soul who
knows the other side of joy?

Near Dawn

Abiding Friend

Abiding Friend,
I am beginning to see
That at this time in my life
I can hold only so much:
Responsibilities, obligations,
Friends, confidants.
In retrospect, I believe
You have sorted through
My life and given to me
Only those few people and
Few responsibilities
That can comfort me
On this journey of grief.
Instead of moaning
That some friends
Have abandoned me,
No longer an intimate
Part of my life,
I must give thanks.
Such friends take up
Too much room.
If they were in my life,
Perhaps I would not have
Room for the
Angels of comfort
That now walk with me.
Time and circumstance
Have changed.
But you have not,
Abiding Friend.

My Neighbor

My neighbor mowed his grass
this morning, and the fragrance
traveled through my window screen.

As I looked out, I saw the clear blue dome of heaven.
I thought of berries from the garden brambles, juice stains
on my fingers. I felt the sun's burn on my neck.

Then, darkness clouded my mind,
for I remembered. I never dreamed my life
would be forever changed, but it is.

My daughter died young.

I Am Here Today

I am here today —
at this point — at this time.
I will not be at this place
tomorrow on grief's journey.
Next week I will be at a new
place: maybe more hollow,
more intense, more devastating,
maybe less. Perhaps, next month,
I'll feel a coolness, just once,
unlike this burning pain.

For now, I am here,
plodding along with sadness,
anxiety, and a tremendous void:
one that can never be filled, one
that will always be part of me.
For now, this moment is mine.

Don't rush me.

Jennifer Pinker

Rain Within

There is rain
in my heart today.
It splatters in the
cracks and broken
places. The wetness
seeps into the
crevices and coats
my heart with a
melancholy gray.
But I am told:
Rain can't get
my soul wet.

Before Breakfast

Tribute to Willa Cather

I woke this morning
startled and uncertain
when her fragrance
suddenly shrouded me.
It floated into
the fissure of my soul.
And I knew that she
was here with me.
Her soft touch,
her gentle voice —
I grasped a bit of her
before the day began —
before breakfast.

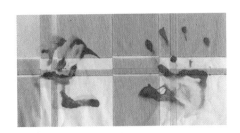

The Mulberry Tree

I wish you could have known me before bare November
when birds sang in the mulberry tree, bows arched
in the wind, and leaves danced the minuet.

Branches pointed skyward, and berries hung with juice.
Those days of summer,
Do you remember?

Laden limbs invited doves and jays to come,
to taste the purple sweetness
of those sun-filled days.

We sat listening to the cooing of the doves
and the chattering of the jays;
all tasted the sweet juice of summer.

I remember that sweet juice of past warm days
and long for that savory sweet tartness on my lips;
yet, I know the berries will never again be as sweet.

One Moment More

In the afternoon gray
when winter touches me,
I think of you and
hold your image
in my heart.
With darkness
all around
I hear gloomy
voices, but your
tone rises clearly
above the din,
and I hold your image
in my heart.
When light seems
only a memory
and hope a
distant stranger,
when the world
spins out of control,
I hold your image
in my heart.
And, then, I live
a moment more.

Jennifer Pinker

Today I Write

Today, I write the saddest lines,
not yesterday or days to come.

For, I read black words in cursive scrawl,
the crayoned words on her bare wall.

I saw a tree-swing standing still,
a seat and rope without a will.

I touched a backpack stained with ink,
a rainbow-time I'd always think.

I saw a golden butterfly
up in the cloudless azure sky.

Today, I can be sad.

Only Words

There are no words, I say,
but words are all I have.
For words begin to tell
the story of great love.
Yet, in my throat, words stick
when they describe my grief,
but words are all I have.

```
P U C K E R E D

CREEK    PERK       CDEEKPRU
CREED    PERKED
CREEP    DUKE
CRUDE    PUKE
DECK     CRUD
DUCK     REED
ECRU     PERCE
DEER     PERCED
PUCK     CURED
PECK     DEUCE
KEEP     PUCKER
PEEK     CRUE
PRUDE    EUKER
CURE     REDUCE
RUDE
```

Layers of Later

When sorrow first came, I had no words.
So I stacked those times of sadness in volumes,
pages gray with grief, layer upon layer.

From time to time I lift a page from one;
sometimes I can read it in my mind,
but most often my heart says:

"No, not today. Let me hold that
page of grief just a little longer.
Tomorrow, try again to voice it in your mind."

All Saints' Day

I met him at her grave.
His truck stopped beside my car.
When I saw him, a smile came to my face;
One came to his as well.
We met unplanned —
We came to talk with her again.
Audible or inaudible words,
She heard our hearts;
She knew our silence.
He placed a truffle at her stone —
His sister. My daughter.
We walked together,
Talked of her,
Talked of others
Who had gone before.
Then, we left, knowing
The absence in our lives,
Yet feeling a closeness.
When grief is shared,
No words are needed
To know such depth of loss
On this Day of Saints.

Turn the Hall Light On

As a kid, when I'd slip
Between my bed sheets,
I'd cover my head;
I feared the dark.
Thoughts of the day
Came galloping across
My mind: nostrils flaring,
Tail flailing in the air;
I felt *it* coming to get me.
It's only
A blowing wind,
A swinging door,
A creaking floor,
I'd tell myself.
But I'd smell the
Foulness of darkness.
I feared the Minotaur;
It trampled and devoured;
It transformed me with fear.
Wait! Turn the hall light on.
Even a tiny light could
Dissipate a galloping monster.
With a little light,
Calm found a way inside.

I'm in the dark, again, Lord.
I carry the day's shadows in my heart;
I feel the bull's hot breath beside me.
I'm alone; I'm afraid,
Lord, turn the hall light on.

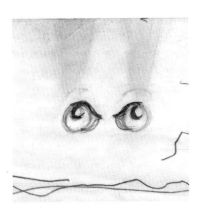

Repack

I didn't pack right
For the journey.
I carried what I thought
I needed: confidence,
Intellect, understanding.
Then, the doctor spoke
In somber tones;
My confidence weakened.
A chemical for cure,
A word I never heard;
My intellect useless.
When sorrow came,
A friend abandoned me;
My understanding failed.

Lord God, I packed
All wrong for my journey.
Strength, hope,
Forgiveness, love —
Help me to repack.

After a Storm

I like the somber, overcast days
after a storm when all of life
steps back and pauses for
a breath. The ground soaks up
the rain and settles comfortably;
the drunken trees stand taller,
more erect and wave their arms
in misty air. Garden vines once
dried and shriveled now yawn
and stretch in damp wetness.
The soul, too, seems refreshed
by witnessing the earth renewed.

I like the gray days of September
when life returns, from tired, old living
if only for a short time.

Jennifer Pinker

Women at Fifty

women at fifty
close doors softly
to rooms that
they will not enter
again.

women at fifty
close the door
to raising children;
for they are gone.
but women remember
the birthing, nurturing,
and growing.

women at fifty
close the door
to strained friendships,
for the closeness
once felt has waned.
what *was* is
in the past.

women at fifty
open the door
to newness;
they stand at the
threshold with
uncertainty and
little expectation.

women at fifty
look ahead and
know the last
door they have
yet to open.

Request

The thought of loss, it never leaves;
The death of her I always grieve.
But like the breeze that moves the trees,
In time, I'll see Your love for me.

The minutes in my days wear long;
I hesitate to move — go on.
Sometimes I think I hear Your voice.
Do You still call my name by choice?

Will You come to me as I pray?
Renew my strength for every day?
Walk beside me when demons rise?
Give me courage to vocalize?

Gentle Father, you know my soul.
I am broken; make me whole.
Come to me, be now my guide.
Come Holy Spirit, in me reside.

Silent, Still Pool

Silent, Still Pool!
rest within me.
noisy days hurt
my ears; they break
my spirit — such days
sear my eyes.
Quiet Pool! stir deeply
within me; gently
heal the wounded parts.
Cleansing Water! wash
the deep places: the
hurt, the broken, the
burned places. And
restore my soul by
your creation,
Still Water!

Juxtaposition

clouds
in the sky will weep
if you do not return
I will sing hymns from
grandma and ballads from The Beatles.
you'll hear my voice
echoing the songs we sang
together
a painter and his brush streak across
the heavens. colors from his pots
softly touch the sky blending afternoon
colors and shapes
if
you no longer laugh
I will laugh for you
on Christmas morning Halloween night
you'll hear me laugh of times
we shared
camel humps and elephant trunks
fill the sky with
what if you do not return?
then I will feel near
you
will be my confidant
my kindred spirit just

as before though now
in solitude
help me to feel you are here
each day
camel humps and elephant trunks
change to seashells scalloping
the misty blue —
paper thin
I fear my memories
will become
only camel humps and elephants trunks
and the sky will weep
just as I.

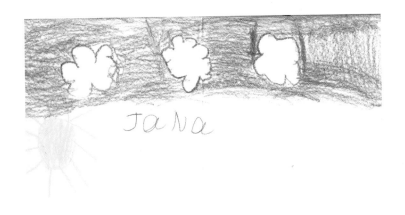

Moving to Dawn

for Roger

Inscribe one's thoughts upon a page,
Imprint one's vision from early age,
The words too dear to speak aloud,
For thoughts come softly as a cloud.

The sound of laughter, who can tell?
Or picture earth's autumn smell?
Or scrawl a tender touch of love?
Or color joy of a youngster's hug?

No wooden words convey such thoughts.
Sound from one's soul is carefully wrought,
That inner place of joy and pain
Where thoughts in reverence remain.

And when these words the heart does speak,
In quietude where souls do meet,
Choose audience with special care
Before a mourner's heart is bare.

For only spirits kindled bright
Can feel the spoken words aright,
Can gently tread on painful space.
The wound once touched now healed by Grace.

Ladder of Hope

I don't need to climb
the ladder of hope all
at one time. I'll get
to the top — one hand
hold at a time. I don't
need to be in a hurry.
I have time —
God's time, not mine.

Goodwill

for Karen

I lost something today,
a little piece of something
in my heart —
deep inside.

I sent a coat away in a
Goodwill bag. Some other
little girl will wear that coat.
She won't be my little girl.
But she will wear part of my girl,
part of my heart, each time
her arms slip through the sleeves.

Today, I sent a coat away.
Did I lose a piece of what I had or
gain a piece of something that
I never had before?

Dance

God invited me to dance,
And I declined.
I said: "I don't know the steps.
The rhythm isn't mine."

So I sat still in solitude
Unhappy, but unmoved.
Without a song,
I wondered and I waited.

I heard a tune,
But not my own.
I swayed with clumsy moves;
I longed to be alone.

And God said: "Stop.
It's not for you.
Listen for music from your soul.
Music comes in different hues."

Then sang a breeze
While in this trance
That stirred a longing.
Can I dance this dance?

Unsure at first,
I took a chance.
Though awkward steps,
I dance the dance.

EPILOGUE

At some point in our lives we are given the task, the privilege, of walking a loved one home. With such a walk, we measure our own steps; we see our own journey, and we believe that death is not the end. When we see our dear one struggle so with living, and then find peace when the struggle ends, we believe that our loving soul is in a place of peace, love, and tranquility. When we see that moment of change, we know the reality of life and death, and we believe in the life beyond.

ABOUT THE AUTHOR

Rebecca Pinker is an adjunct professor of English at Johnson County Community College, Overland Park, Kansas. She completed her undergraduate studies at Capital University (Ohio) and earned her Master's and Ph.D. degrees from the University of Kansas. She is the mother of three children.

ABOUT THE ILLUSTRATOR

Jana Pinker lived to the age of nineteen before losing her battle with liver cancer. Throughout her life, she created the artwork found in this book, selected to augment Rebecca's poetry.